Beautiful Butterflies
Address Book with email and birthdays

Printed in the United States

ISBN-13: 978-1519752659

ISBN-10: 1519752652

This book belongs to: _____

If found please call:_____

Email:_____

© *Marisha - Fotolia.com*

© umnola - Fotolia.com

Name		
Address		
City	State	Zip
Email		
Home Phone	Work Phone	
Cell	Birthday	

Name		
Address		
City	State	Zip
Email		
Home Phone	Work Phone	
Cell	Birthday	

Name		
Address		
City	State	Zip
Email		
Home Phone	Work Phone	
Cell	Birthday	

Name		
Address		
City	State	Zip
Email		
Home Phone	Work Phone	
Cell	Birthday	

A

Name	
Address	
City	State Zip
Email	
Home Phone	Work Phone
Cell	Birthday

Name	
Address	
City	State Zip
Email	
Home Phone	Work Phone
Cell	Birthday

Name	
Address	
City	State Zip
Email	
Home Phone	Work Phone
Cell	Birthday

Name	
Address	
City	State Zip
Email	
Home Phone	Work Phone
Cell	Birthday

Name	
Address	
City	State Zip
Email	
Home Phone	Work Phone
Cell	Birthday

Name	
Address	
City	State Zip
Email	
Home Phone	Work Phone
Cell	Birthday

Name	
Address	
City	State Zip
Email	
Home Phone	Work Phone
Cell	Birthday

Name	
Address	
City	State Zip
Email	
Home Phone	Work Phone
Cell	Birthday

B

Name	
Address	
City	State Zip
Email	
Home Phone	Work Phone
Cell	Birthday

Name	
Address	
City	State Zip
Email	
Home Phone	Work Phone
Cell	Birthday

Name	
Address	
City	State Zip
Email	
Home Phone	Work Phone
Cell	Birthday

Name	
Address	
City	State Zip
Email	
Home Phone	Work Phone
Cell	Birthday

Name	
Address	
City	State Zip
Email	
Home Phone	Work Phone
Cell	Birthday

Name	
Address	
City	State Zip
Email	
Home Phone	Work Phone
Cell	Birthday

Name	
Address	
City	State Zip
Email	
Home Phone	Work Phone
Cell	Birthday

Name	
Address	
City	State Zip
Email	
Home Phone	Work Phone
Cell	Birthday

Name	
Address	
City	State Zip
Email	
Home Phone	Work Phone
Cell	Birthday

Name	
Address	
City	State Zip
Email	
Home Phone	Work Phone
Cell	Birthday

Name	
Address	
City	State Zip
Email	
Home Phone	Work Phone
Cell	Birthday

Name	
Address	
City	State Zip
Email	
Home Phone	Work Phone
Cell	Birthday

D

Name	
Address	
City	State Zip
Email	
Home Phone	Work Phone
Cell	Birthday

Name	
Address	
City	State Zip
Email	
Home Phone	Work Phone
Cell	Birthday

Name	
Address	
City	State Zip
Email	
Home Phone	Work Phone
Cell	Birthday

Name	
Address	
City	State Zip
Email	
Home Phone	Work Phone
Cell	Birthday

D

Name	
Address	
City	State Zip
Email	
Home Phone	Work Phone
Cell	Birthday

Name	
Address	
City	State Zip
Email	
Home Phone	Work Phone
Cell	Birthday

Name	
Address	
City	State Zip
Email	
Home Phone	Work Phone
Cell	Birthday

Name	
Address	
City	State Zip
Email	
Home Phone	Work Phone
Cell	Birthday

Name	
Address	
City	State Zip
Email	
Home Phone	Work Phone
Cell	Birthday

Name	
Address	
City	State Zip
Email	
Home Phone	Work Phone
Cell	Birthday

Name	
Address	
City	State Zip
Email	
Home Phone	Work Phone
Cell	Birthday

Name	
Address	
City	State Zip
Email	
Home Phone	Work Phone
Cell	Birthday

E

Name	
Address	
City	State Zip
Email	
Home Phone	Work Phone
Cell	Birthday

Name	
Address	
City	State Zip
Email	
Home Phone	Work Phone
Cell	Birthday

Name	
Address	
City	State Zip
Email	
Home Phone	Work Phone
Cell	Birthday

Name	
Address	
City	State Zip
Email	
Home Phone	Work Phone
Cell	Birthday

F

Name	
Address	
City	State Zip
Email	
Home Phone	Work Phone
Cell	Birthday

Name	
Address	
City	State Zip
Email	
Home Phone	Work Phone
Cell	Birthday

Name	
Address	
City	State Zip
Email	
Home Phone	Work Phone
Cell	Birthday

Name	
Address	
City	State Zip
Email	
Home Phone	Work Phone
Cell	Birthday

F

Name	
Address	
City	State Zip
Email	
Home Phone	Work Phone
Cell	Birthday

Name	
Address	
City	State Zip
Email	
Home Phone	Work Phone
Cell	Birthday

Name	
Address	
City	State Zip
Email	
Home Phone	Work Phone
Cell	Birthday

Name	
Address	
City	State Zip
Email	
Home Phone	Work Phone
Cell	Birthday

Name		
Address		
City	State	Zip
Email		
Home Phone	Work Phone	
Cell	Birthday	

Name		
Address		
City	State	Zip
Email		
Home Phone	Work Phone	
Cell	Birthday	

Name		
Address		
City	State	Zip
Email		
Home Phone	Work Phone	
Cell	Birthday	

Name		
Address		
City	State	Zip
Email		
Home Phone	Work Phone	
Cell	Birthday	

Name	
Address	
City	State Zip
Email	
Home Phone	Work Phone
Cell	Birthday

Name	
Address	
City	State Zip
Email	
Home Phone	Work Phone
Cell	Birthday

Name	
Address	
City	State Zip
Email	
Home Phone	Work Phone
Cell	Birthday

Name	
Address	
City	State Zip
Email	
Home Phone	Work Phone
Cell	Birthday

Name	
Address	
City	State Zip
Email	
Home Phone	Work Phone
Cell	Birthday

Name	
Address	
City	State Zip
Email	
Home Phone	Work Phone
Cell	Birthday

Name	
Address	
City	State Zip
Email	
Home Phone	Work Phone
Cell	Birthday

Name	
Address	
City	State Zip
Email	
Home Phone	Work Phone
Cell	Birthday

Name	
Address	
City	State Zip
Email	
Home Phone	Work Phone
Cell	Birthday

Name	
Address	
City	State Zip
Email	
Home Phone	Work Phone
Cell	Birthday

Name	
Address	
City	State Zip
Email	
Home Phone	Work Phone
Cell	Birthday

Name	
Address	
City	State Zip
Email	
Home Phone	Work Phone
Cell	Birthday

Name		
Address		
City	State	Zip
Email		
Home Phone	Work Phone	
Cell	Birthday	

Name		
Address		
City	State	Zip
Email		
Home Phone	Work Phone	
Cell	Birthday	

Name		
Address		
City	State	Zip
Email		
Home Phone	Work Phone	
Cell	Birthday	

Name		
Address		
City	State	Zip
Email		
Home Phone	Work Phone	
Cell	Birthday	

Name	
Address	
City	State Zip
Email	
Home Phone	Work Phone
Cell	Birthday

Name	
Address	
City	State Zip
Email	
Home Phone	Work Phone
Cell	Birthday

Name	
Address	
City	State Zip
Email	
Home Phone	Work Phone
Cell	Birthday

Name	
Address	
City	State Zip
Email	
Home Phone	Work Phone
Cell	Birthday

J

Name	
Address	
City	State Zip
Email	
Home Phone	Work Phone
Cell	Birthday

Name	
Address	
City	State Zip
Email	
Home Phone	Work Phone
Cell	Birthday

Name	
Address	
City	State Zip
Email	
Home Phone	Work Phone
Cell	Birthday

Name	
Address	
City	State Zip
Email	
Home Phone	Work Phone
Cell	Birthday

J

Name		
Address		
City	State	Zip
Email		
Home Phone	Work Phone	
Cell	Birthday	

Name		
Address		
City	State	Zip
Email		
Home Phone	Work Phone	
Cell	Birthday	

Name		
Address		
City	State	Zip
Email		
Home Phone	Work Phone	
Cell	Birthday	

Name		
Address		
City	State	Zip
Email		
Home Phone	Work Phone	
Cell	Birthday	

Name	
Address	
City	State Zip
Email	
Home Phone	Work Phone
Cell	Birthday

Name	
Address	
City	State Zip
Email	
Home Phone	Work Phone
Cell	Birthday

Name	
Address	
City	State Zip
Email	
Home Phone	Work Phone
Cell	Birthday

Name	
Address	
City	State Zip
Email	
Home Phone	Work Phone
Cell	Birthday

Name		
Address		
City	State	Zip
Email		
Home Phone	Work Phone	
Cell	Birthday	

Name		
Address		
City	State	Zip
Email		
Home Phone	Work Phone	
Cell	Birthday	

Name		
Address		
City	State	Zip
Email		
Home Phone	Work Phone	
Cell	Birthday	

Name		
Address		
City	State	Zip
Email		
Home Phone	Work Phone	
Cell	Birthday	

Name	
Address	
City	State　　　Zip
Email	
Home Phone	Work Phone
Cell	Birthday

Name	
Address	
City	State　　　Zip
Email	
Home Phone	Work Phone
Cell	Birthday

Name	
Address	
City	State　　　Zip
Email	
Home Phone	Work Phone
Cell	Birthday

Name	
Address	
City	State　　　Zip
Email	
Home Phone	Work Phone
Cell	Birthday

L

Name	
Address	
City	State Zip
Email	
Home Phone	Work Phone
Cell	Birthday

Name	
Address	
City	State Zip
Email	
Home Phone	Work Phone
Cell	Birthday

Name	
Address	
City	State Zip
Email	
Home Phone	Work Phone
Cell	Birthday

Name	
Address	
City	State Zip
Email	
Home Phone	Work Phone
Cell	Birthday

Name		
Address		
City	State	Zip
Email		
Home Phone	Work Phone	
Cell	Birthday	

Name		
Address		
City	State	Zip
Email		
Home Phone	Work Phone	
Cell	Birthday	

Name		
Address		
City	State	Zip
Email		
Home Phone	Work Phone	
Cell	Birthday	

Name		
Address		
City	State	Zip
Email		
Home Phone	Work Phone	
Cell	Birthday	

Name	
Address	
City	State Zip
Email	
Home Phone	Work Phone
Cell	Birthday

Name	
Address	
City	State Zip
Email	
Home Phone	Work Phone
Cell	Birthday

Name	
Address	
City	State Zip
Email	
Home Phone	Work Phone
Cell	Birthday

Name	
Address	
City	State Zip
Email	
Home Phone	Work Phone
Cell	Birthday

Name	
Address	
City	State Zip
Email	
Home Phone	Work Phone
Cell	Birthday

Name	
Address	
City	State Zip
Email	
Home Phone	Work Phone
Cell	Birthday

Name	
Address	
City	State Zip
Email	
Home Phone	Work Phone
Cell	Birthday

Name	
Address	
City	State Zip
Email	
Home Phone	Work Phone
Cell	Birthday

Name	
Address	
City	State Zip
Email	
Home Phone	Work Phone
Cell	Birthday

Name	
Address	
City	State Zip
Email	
Home Phone	Work Phone
Cell	Birthday

Name	
Address	
City	State Zip
Email	
Home Phone	Work Phone
Cell	Birthday

Name	
Address	
City	State Zip
Email	
Home Phone	Work Phone
Cell	Birthday

Name	
Address	
City	State Zip
Email	
Home Phone	Work Phone
Cell	Birthday

Name	
Address	
City	State Zip
Email	
Home Phone	Work Phone
Cell	Birthday

Name	
Address	
City	State Zip
Email	
Home Phone	Work Phone
Cell	Birthday

Name	
Address	
City	State Zip
Email	
Home Phone	Work Phone
Cell	Birthday

Name		
Address		
City	State	Zip
Email		
Home Phone	Work Phone	
Cell	Birthday	

Name		
Address		
City	State	Zip
Email		
Home Phone	Work Phone	
Cell	Birthday	

Name		
Address		
City	State	Zip
Email		
Home Phone	Work Phone	
Cell	Birthday	

Name		
Address		
City	State	Zip
Email		
Home Phone	Work Phone	
Cell	Birthday	

P

Name	
Address	
City	State Zip
Email	
Home Phone	Work Phone
Cell	Birthday

Name	
Address	
City	State Zip
Email	
Home Phone	Work Phone
Cell	Birthday

Name	
Address	
City	State Zip
Email	
Home Phone	Work Phone
Cell	Birthday

Name	
Address	
City	State Zip
Email	
Home Phone	Work Phone
Cell	Birthday

P

Name	
Address	
City	State Zip
Email	
Home Phone	Work Phone
Cell	Birthday

Name	
Address	
City	State Zip
Email	
Home Phone	Work Phone
Cell	Birthday

Name	
Address	
City	State Zip
Email	
Home Phone	Work Phone
Cell	Birthday

Name	
Address	
City	State Zip
Email	
Home Phone	Work Phone
Cell	Birthday

Name	
Address	
City	State Zip
Email	
Home Phone	Work Phone
Cell	Birthday

Name	
Address	
City	State Zip
Email	
Home Phone	Work Phone
Cell	Birthday

Name	
Address	
City	State Zip
Email	
Home Phone	Work Phone
Cell	Birthday

Name	
Address	
City	State Zip
Email	
Home Phone	Work Phone
Cell	Birthday

Name	
Address	
City	State Zip
Email	
Home Phone	Work Phone
Cell	Birthday

Name	
Address	
City	State Zip
Email	
Home Phone	Work Phone
Cell	Birthday

Name	
Address	
City	State Zip
Email	
Home Phone	Work Phone
Cell	Birthday

Name	
Address	
City	State Zip
Email	
Home Phone	Work Phone
Cell	Birthday

Name		
Address		
City	State	Zip
Email		
Home Phone	Work Phone	
Cell	Birthday	

Name		
Address		
City	State	Zip
Email		
Home Phone	Work Phone	
Cell	Birthday	

Name		
Address		
City	State	Zip
Email		
Home Phone	Work Phone	
Cell	Birthday	

Name		
Address		
City	State	Zip
Email		
Home Phone	Work Phone	
Cell	Birthday	

Name	
Address	
City	State Zip
Email	
Home Phone	Work Phone
Cell	Birthday

Name	
Address	
City	State Zip
Email	
Home Phone	Work Phone
Cell	Birthday

Name	
Address	
City	State Zip
Email	
Home Phone	Work Phone
Cell	Birthday

Name	
Address	
City	State Zip
Email	
Home Phone	Work Phone
Cell	Birthday

Name	
Address	
City	State Zip
Email	
Home Phone	Work Phone
Cell	Birthday

Name	
Address	
City	State Zip
Email	
Home Phone	Work Phone
Cell	Birthday

Name	
Address	
City	State Zip
Email	
Home Phone	Work Phone
Cell	Birthday

Name	
Address	
City	State Zip
Email	
Home Phone	Work Phone
Cell	Birthday

S

Name	
Address	
City	State Zip
Email	
Home Phone	Work Phone
Cell	Birthday

Name	
Address	
City	State Zip
Email	
Home Phone	Work Phone
Cell	Birthday

Name	
Address	
City	State Zip
Email	
Home Phone	Work Phone
Cell	Birthday

Name	
Address	
City	State Zip
Email	
Home Phone	Work Phone
Cell	Birthday

Name		
Address		
City	State	Zip
Email		
Home Phone	Work Phone	
Cell	Birthday	

Name		
Address		
City	State	Zip
Email		
Home Phone	Work Phone	
Cell	Birthday	

Name		
Address		
City	State	Zip
Email		
Home Phone	Work Phone	
Cell	Birthday	

Name		
Address		
City	State	Zip
Email		
Home Phone	Work Phone	
Cell	Birthday	

Name	
Address	
City	State Zip
Email	
Home Phone	Work Phone
Cell	Birthday

Name	
Address	
City	State Zip
Email	
Home Phone	Work Phone
Cell	Birthday

Name	
Address	
City	State Zip
Email	
Home Phone	Work Phone
Cell	Birthday

Name	
Address	
City	State Zip
Email	
Home Phone	Work Phone
Cell	Birthday

Name		
Address		
City	State	Zip
Email		
Home Phone	Work Phone	
Cell	Birthday	

Name		
Address		
City	State	Zip
Email		
Home Phone	Work Phone	
Cell	Birthday	

Name		
Address		
City	State	Zip
Email		
Home Phone	Work Phone	
Cell	Birthday	

Name		
Address		
City	State	Zip
Email		
Home Phone	Work Phone	
Cell	Birthday	

Name	
Address	
City	State Zip
Email	
Home Phone	Work Phone
Cell	Birthday

Name	
Address	
City	State Zip
Email	
Home Phone	Work Phone
Cell	Birthday

Name	
Address	
City	State Zip
Email	
Home Phone	Work Phone
Cell	Birthday

Name	
Address	
City	State Zip
Email	
Home Phone	Work Phone
Cell	Birthday

Name	
Address	
City	State Zip
Email	
Home Phone	Work Phone
Cell	Birthday

Name	
Address	
City	State Zip
Email	
Home Phone	Work Phone
Cell	Birthday

Name	
Address	
City	State Zip
Email	
Home Phone	Work Phone
Cell	Birthday

Name	
Address	
City	State Zip
Email	
Home Phone	Work Phone
Cell	Birthday

Name	
Address	
City	State Zip
Email	
Home Phone	Work Phone
Cell	Birthday

Name	
Address	
City	State Zip
Email	
Home Phone	Work Phone
Cell	Birthday

Name	
Address	
City	State Zip
Email	
Home Phone	Work Phone
Cell	Birthday

Name	
Address	
City	State Zip
Email	
Home Phone	Work Phone
Cell	Birthday

Name		
Address		
City	State	Zip
Email		
Home Phone	Work Phone	
Cell	Birthday	

Name		
Address		
City	State	Zip
Email		
Home Phone	Work Phone	
Cell	Birthday	

Name		
Address		
City	State	Zip
Email		
Home Phone	Work Phone	
Cell	Birthday	

Name		
Address		
City	State	Zip
Email		
Home Phone	Work Phone	
Cell	Birthday	

Name	
Address	
City	State Zip
Email	
Home Phone	Work Phone
Cell	Birthday

Name	
Address	
City	State Zip
Email	
Home Phone	Work Phone
Cell	Birthday

Name	
Address	
City	State Zip
Email	
Home Phone	Work Phone
Cell	Birthday

Name	
Address	
City	State Zip
Email	
Home Phone	Work Phone
Cell	Birthday

XYZ

Name	
Address	
City	State Zip
Email	
Home Phone	Work Phone
Cell	Birthday

Name	
Address	
City	State Zip
Email	
Home Phone	Work Phone
Cell	Birthday

Name	
Address	
City	State Zip
Email	
Home Phone	Work Phone
Cell	Birthday

Name	
Address	
City	State Zip
Email	
Home Phone	Work Phone
Cell	Birthday

XYZ

Name	
Address	
City	State Zip
Email	
Home Phone	Work Phone
Cell	Birthday

Name	
Address	
City	State Zip
Email	
Home Phone	Work Phone
Cell	Birthday

Name	
Address	
City	State Zip
Email	
Home Phone	Work Phone
Cell	Birthday

Name	
Address	
City	State Zip
Email	
Home Phone	Work Phone
Cell	Birthday

All Write All Bright Books
71 Tandy Lane
Sparta, TN 38583
(931) 946-1221

16161993R00030

Printed in Great Britain
by Amazon